CVJC

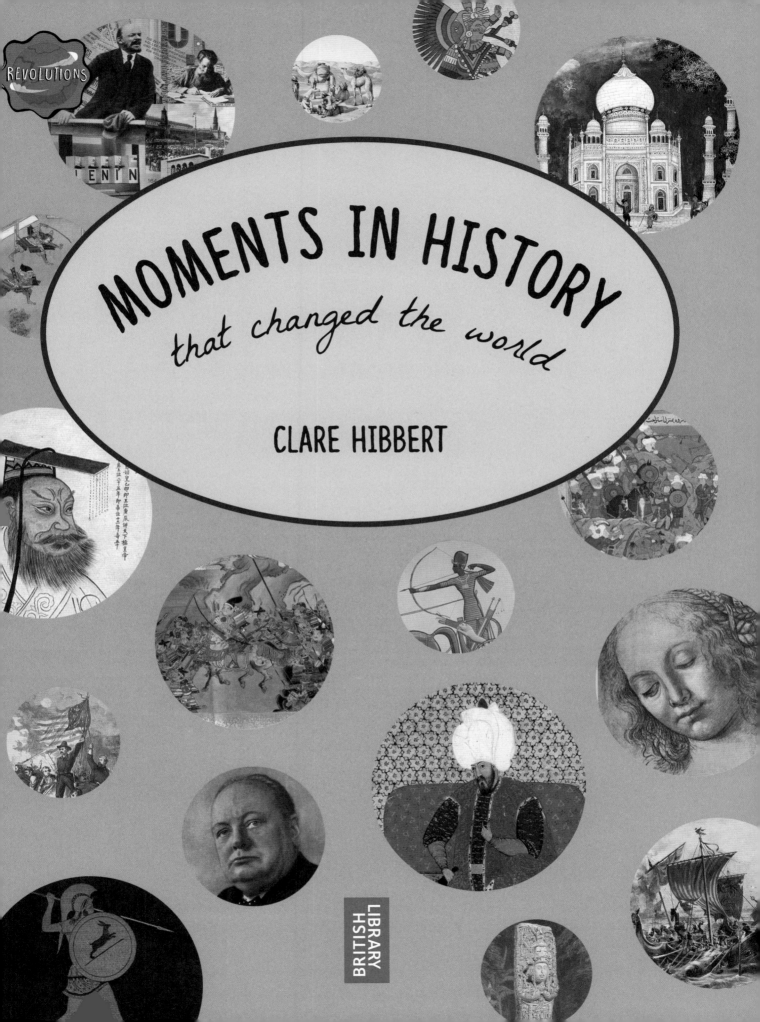

REVOLUTIONS

MOMENTS IN HISTORY
that changed the world

CLARE HIBBERT

BRITISH LIBRARY

First published 2017 by
The British Library
96 Euston Road
London NW1 2DB

ISBN 978 0 7123 5670 1

British Library Cataloguing in Publication Data
A catalogue record for this publication is available
from the British Library

Designed by Amy McSimpson @ Hollow Pond
Picture research by Sally Nicholls

Printed in China by C&C Offset Printing Co.

MOMENTS IN HISTORY
that changed the world

INTRODUCTION

The story of modern humans began before written history. It is 100,000 years since our species, *Homo sapiens*, spread out from Africa. Back then, we had simple shelters, stone tools and we ate what we could find or kill. Today, we live in advanced societies. This book looks at a few of the key moments along our journey.

Battling a shared enemy can help to bring people closer together.

CONFLICTS

Throughout history, humans have fought each other. We have tussled over land or simply to show off our importance. We have also battled about ideas. Wars cost lives, but they also sometimes bring about changes for the better.

People who fight for freedom have to think hard about the society they want to build.

Many new inventions and medical advances often happen during wartime.

ACHIEVEMENTS

Humans are big-brained and adaptable. We learn from our successes. Along our journey we have created ordered societies with leaders and laws. Scientists and artists have built on each tiny advance made by earlier generations.

Trying out new ideas, such as giving people a vote, can help to make society fairer.

Writing and other communications allow us to share ideas.

Beautiful monuments help to inspire the people who follow after.

The more peoples and lands that we encounter, the more we learn from each other.

 Look out for these boxes. They introduce you to very important people from history.

NEED TO KNOW

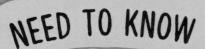

Find out key facts and dates in these boxes.

2.5 MYA – 500 CE

PREHISTORY TO THE CLASSICAL AGE

One of the first human species, *Homo habilis*, evolved in Africa around 2.5 million years ago (mya). It used tools and could make fire. Today we *Homo sapiens* are the only human species. When we first migrated out of Africa, we lived as simple hunter-gatherers.

BECOMING CIVILISED

Living settled lives as farmers was the first step towards civilised society. Soon villages grew into towns and cities. The first arose in the Indus Valley, Mesopotamia and Egypt. These early civilisations had kings and belief systems. They developed writing. Soon they also learned how to work metal. Later Bronze Age cultures included the Greeks, Persians and Romans.

These clay seals found at Harappa in the Indus Valley date to around 3250 BCE. They seem to show picture writing.

Early hunter-gatherers created the first art. These lions were painted on the walls of Chauvet Cave, in southern France, around 30,000 years ago.

THE FIRST CITIES

People learned to farm around 9500 BCE in the area that we call the Middle East. Farming produced more food than hunting and gathering. It left people free to do other jobs, such as making leather or metalworking. Over time, farming villages grew into cities with grand buildings.

This colourful sketch shows the palace of King Sennacherib at Nineveh. It was built around 700 BCE.

VIP This model displays the jewels and headdress of the Sumerian queen Puabi, who lived in the city of Ur.

NEED TO KNOW

The Sumerians built the first cities, such as Ur. They lived in southern Mesopotamia (modern-day Iraq) around 2500 BCE.

The Assyrians ruled a mighty empire that covered all of Mesopotamia around the 800s BCE. Their capital city was Nineveh.

There were two Babylonian empires — one before the Assyrians, in the 1700s and 1600s BCE, and one after, during the 600s and 500s BCE.

SIGNS OF CIVILISATION

Those first cities in Mesopotamia had advanced societies. There were leaders and laws, inventors and scientists, merchants and soldiers, artists and priests. Religious beliefs, customs and traditions helped people to cope with the mysteries of the world.

An Assyrian priest wearing earrings and a decorative headband

Shamash, the sun god

Hammurabi, king of Babylon from 1792 to 1750 BCE

This black stone lists Babylon's laws ... and the punishments for disobeying them.

THE BIRTH OF WRITING

People had communicated by speaking since prehistoric times, but now they needed to write and keep records. The Sumerians came up with the first writing system – wedge-shaped marks called cuneiform. Later Mesopotamian peoples adopted cuneiform, too.

Cuneiform tablet from around 2000 BCE

Marks have been pressed into wet clay with a stylus.

REVOLUTIONS

Discoveries made long ago in those first cities still influence us today. The Mesopotamians had writing, maths and laws set in stone.

LAND OF THE PYRAMIDS

There was a great civilisation in ancient Egypt for thousands of years. It is famous for its pyramids - huge, triangular tombs that held dead pharaohs (kings) and the treasures they would need in the afterlife. But tomb robbers raided the pyramids. Later Egyptian royals were buried in hidden, underground tombs instead.

This golden case held the mummy (preserved body) of a young pharaoh called Tutankhamun. His underground tomb was found in 1922.

Crook and flail are signs of protection and power.

Funeral barge, carrying the dead pharaoh

NEED TO KNOW

VIP Ramesses II fought and won wars. He built many temples and monuments.

The tallest pyramid is the Great Pyramid at Giza. When it was finished in **2560** BCE, it stood **146** m (**481** ft) tall.

From **1550** to **1050** BCE, pharaohs and nobles were buried in the Valley of the Kings and Valley of the Queens, near Thebes.

Egypt was at the height of its power in the **1200s** BCE, during the reign of Ramesses II.

EGYPTIAN EXPERTISE

The Egyptians were not only great architects. They had armies, ships and courts of law. Their craftworkers made beautiful objects. Their priests studied the Moon and stars. They worked out a calendar so that farmers knew when to plant their crops.

The Karnak temple complex shows the Egyptians' astronomy knowhow. Its pillars lined up with the positions of the stars or Sun at important times of the year.

WOW!

The Great Pyramid was built with about 2.3 million stone blocks.

Each picture stands for an object, idea a sound.

Osiris, god of death

Anubis, god of mummy-making

Horus, the sky god

PAPER AND WRITING

Our word 'paper' comes from papyrus, a tall reed that grows by the Nile. The Egyptians used its fibres to make the first paper. They also came up with a writing system using pictures, called hieroglyphs.

Hieroglyphs survive on papyrus scrolls, wall paintings (here) and stone monuments.

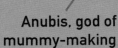

REVOLUTIONS

Egypt's buildings inspire and puzzle us, because they were built without machines. Its myths and art influenced later cultures, too.

RULE BY THE PEOPLE

Ancient Greece was made up of a number of city-states, each with its own government. Some, such as Sparta and Corinth, were ruled by kings. Others, such as Athens and Thebes, were ruled by the people. Our word democracy is Greek for 'rule by the people'.

Politicians met in this building. They ruled on behalf of the people.

Citizens gathered to talk and vote in the *agora* (marketplace) in the centre of Athens.

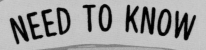

Citizens could throw a politician out of the city by carving his name on a piece of pottery.

The Athenians' most famous leader was Pericles, who governed in the 400s BCE.

NEED TO KNOW

VIP

According to legend, a king called Theseus founded Athens around **3000** BCE. The city-state became a democracy around **508** BCE.

Athens was most powerful from **480** to **404** BCE. Many of its greatest leaders, thinkers, playwrights and historians lived then, and its finest buildings were built.

Alexander the Great ended Greek democracy around **322** BCE. King of the city-state of Macedon, he soon conquered the rest of Greece and ruled over a vast empire.

PEOPLE POWER

In today's democracies, all adults can vote. In ancient Athens, only citizens could. Citizens were free men who had been born in Athens. Women and slaves had no say in how the state was run, and neither did non-Athenian men.

Voting came at a price. Every citizen had to fight for his city-state.

WOW!

Any citizen could speak at meetings in the agora. A sand timer stopped anyone waffling on for too long.

VIOLENT TIMES

The Greek city-states banded together to fight the Persians between 499 BCE and 449 BCE. The Persians wanted their land. But once the city-states did not have a shared enemy, they were not so friendly to each other. Athens and Sparta warred from 431 to 404 BCE.

King Leonidas of Sparta helped to see off the Persians when they tried to invade in 480 BCE.

REVOLUTIONS

Most states today are democracies. We also still believe Greek discoveries about maths, science and philosophy (ideas) — and enjoy their gripping stories of heroes and monsters.

POWERFUL PERSIA

Persia (modern-day Iran) was Greece's neighbour ... and its fierce rival for land and power. During the 400s BCE, the Persians tried to conquer Greece twice. They failed, but they did manage to build a huge and powerful empire. At the time, Persia contained about half of the world's total population!

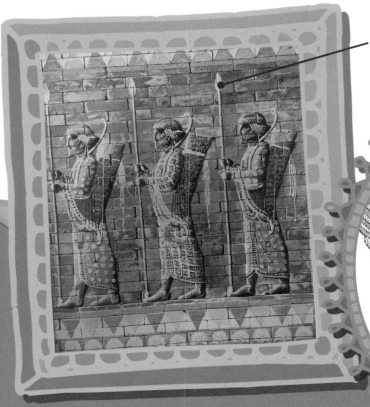

The Persian empire was built on military might. This mosaic at Susa shows a trio of Persian soldiers, each armed with a spear, bow and arrows.

Cyrus the Great inherited a small kingdom in southern Iran in 559 BCE. His armies conquered neighbouring lands and peoples to create the Persian empire.

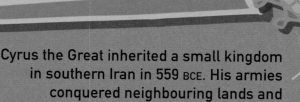

NEED TO KNOW

VIP

Darius I ruled from 522 to 486 BCE. He built a new capital at Persepolis.

Cyrus the Great was king from 559 to 530 BCE. In 547 BCE, he conquered much of Anatolia (modern-day Turkey).

Darius I of Persia went to war against the Greeks after they helped the people of Anatolia to revolt. He was defeated at Marathon in 490 BCE.

Like the Greek city-states, the Persian empire could not withstand Alexander the Great. By 330 BCE he had conquered all of Persia.

MIGHTY PERSEPOLIS

By the reign of Darius I, the empire stretched from Egypt and Thrace (southeast Balkans) in the west to Afghanistan in the east. The city of Persepolis was built to show off Persia's might. It had splendid gateways and grand halls, with pillars and statues, mosaics and wall reliefs.

Modern marathon races are inspired by a messenger who ran from Marathon to Athens — a distance of 40 km (25 miles) — with news of the Greek victory.

This 19th-century drawing shows one of the gateways at Persepolis.

This is a guardian angel called a faravahar. It comes from Zoroastrianism, the religion of ancient Persia.

ALL ABOUT REVENGE

Darius I suffered a terrible defeat at Marathon, even though he had 25,000 foot soldiers and the Greeks had only 10,000. Ten years later his son Xerxes invaded Greece, hoping to teach the Greeks a lesson. He burned the city of Athens, but was soon sent packing.

Xerxes marched into Greece in 480 BCE.

This is the monumental gateway of Xerxes at Persepolis.

REVOLUTIONS

For the proportion of the world's people it controlled, Persia was the biggest empire ever! Its religion, Zoroastrianism, influenced other belief systems, such as Judaism.

THE BIRTH OF CHINA

From around 475 to 221 BCE China was made up of seven states that were constantly at war with each other. That all changed when Zheng became king of the state of Qin. By 221 BCE, he had conquered the other six states and declared himself China's 'First Emperor'.

When he died, Qin Shi Huangdi was buried with an army of thousands of life-size terracotta (clay) soldiers.

Zheng renamed himself Qin Shi Huangdi ('First Emperor of Qin').

NEED TO KNOW

Wen was the first of the Zhou kings. His son Wu defeated the Shang.

The Shang dynasty ruled northeastern China from **1600** BCE for more than five centuries.

In **1046** BCE, the Zhou overthrew the Shang. They lost control of their kingdom around **771** BCE, and that's when the Warring States time began.

The Qin dynasty lasted from **221** to **206** BCE. Next came the Han dynasty, founded by a peasant called Liu Bang.

THE GREAT WALL

Qin Shi Huangdi created the first Great Wall China by joining up existing defensive walls. Hardly any of that original wall remains. The parts that still stand today were built just over 600 years ago.

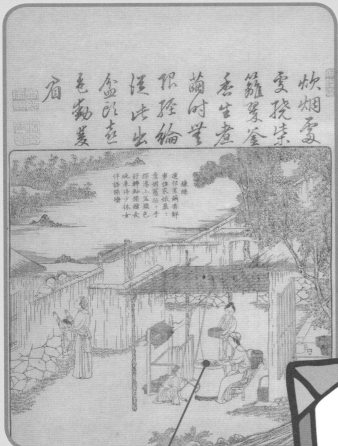

There were watchtowers or lookout posts along the wall.

The 21,200-km (13,170-mile) Great Wall was rebuilt in stone and brick during the Ming dynasty.

Qin Shi Huangdi boasted that his dynasty would rule for 10,000 generations. It lasted 15 years.

PRECIOUS SILK

According to legend, the Chinese discovered how to make silk as early as 3000 BCE. By the time of the Han dynasty, there was a proper trade route linking China to the West as far as Rome. It was known as the Silk Road.

This 17th-century illustration shows women winding strands of silk onto reels.

REVOLUTIONS

Qin Shi Huangdi laid the foundations for an organised empire. He gave coins, weights and measures standard values. He standardised Chinese writing, too.

MURDER IN ROME

Rome was one of the great ancient civilisations. It began life as a city-state ruled by kings. Then it was a republic for 500 years, ruled by its people. The republic collapsed after the brutal murder of famous leader Julius Caesar in 43 BCE. Rome went on to become an empire, ruled by emperors.

Caesar was a military man. In the five years before his death he was busy trying to strengthen Rome's power.

Caesar was killed in the Roman Senate House. The senators stabbed him more than 20 times.

A 15th-century illustration of Rome's first emperor, Augustus, holding a sceptre and sword.

NEED TO KNOW

VIP

Tarquin the Proud was the last king of Rome. His people revolted against him in **509** BCE because he was so full of himself.

Civil wars followed Caesar's assassination. Then, in **27** BCE, his adopted son Augustus became Rome's first emperor.

The last Roman emperor in the West was Romulus Augustulus. Barbarians threw him out in **476** CE.

Romulus and Remus had been raised by a wolf.

The Romans believed that Romulus and Remus's father was Mars, the god of war.

STRANGE BEGINNINGS

According to legend, Rome was founded by twin brothers, Romulus and Remus. The pair fought about exactly where to build the city, and Remus was killed. Romulus was the city-state's first king.

SUPER CIVILISATION

The Romans were skilled engineers. They built roads, aqueducts and fine buildings. Rich people's homes even had underfloor heating. Every Roman town had at least one public baths, where people went to socialise as well as to get clean.

The magnificent Baths of Caracalla were built in Rome in the 210s CE. There were rooms with cold, warm and hot pools.

REVOLUTIONS

At its height, the Roman empire stretched from Spain in the west to Syria in the east. Its beliefs and customs spread across the known world.

500 CE – 1350

MEDIEVAL TIMES

When the Roman empire collapsed in the West, it took time for Europe to recover. The Christian Church grew powerful; Islam was born and spread across the Middle East, Africa and Europe. The civilisations of China and Japan flourished in the East, and the Maya and Aztecs in South America.

THE DARK AGES

The time just after the end of the Roman empire is sometimes called Europe's Dark Ages. It was a period of change. New kingdoms and empires emerged. Religions helped to spread books, learning, architecture and art. Everyone knew their place and that made society more stable. However, people also had to face terrible disasters such as famine, wars and plague.

In medieval Europe, society was organised so that peasants and knights served their lords, and lords served their kings. There was a similar system in Japan, where the knightly class were called samurai.

Nations were born or grew because of wars and invasions. The Mongols of Central Asia captured lands in both Europe and Asia.

ABANDONED CITIES

The Maya lived in the forests of Central America. Like the Greeks, they had powerful city-states. They built amazing temples and worshipped many gods. They developed their own writing system, and their astronomers were knowledgeable about the movements of the Sun, Moon, planets and stars.

This drawing shows a ruined Mayan temple, discovered in the 19th century.

Each city-state had its own ruler. This is a statue of Lord Eighteen Rabbit, king of Copán from 695 to 738 CE.

 **VIP** Pakal ruled Palenque from 615 to 683 CE. He was only 12 years old when he became king!

NEED TO KNOW

The Maya lived as settled farmers from around **4250** BCE. Their civilisation was at its height from **250** CE to **900** CE.

No one is sure why, but many great Mayan cities were abandoned around **900** CE. They included Palenque, Tikal and Copán.

Mayan culture carried on in parts of Mexico, for example at Uxmal and Chichén Itzá, until the Spanish conquistadors (conquerors) arrived around **1500**.

WONDERFUL WORDS

The Maya wrote using pictures called hieroglyphs. They carved them into stone or painted them on bark paper, wood or pottery. They could also write any number by combining just three symbols – shells, dots and lines.

A page from a Mayan book written on fig-tree bark

The Maya used combinations of shells, dots and lines to write their numbers. A line with two dots over it signified the number 7 (the line means 5 and the dots make 2).

MAYAN MYSTERY

It is hard to imagine how a great civilisation can fizzle out. Perhaps a terrible disease struck the Maya or they rose up against their kings. Perhaps the Maya became part of other civilisations, such as the Aztecs. Their last remaining city-states crumbled when the Spanish arrived. Many Maya retreated into the forest to be farmers.

Mayan gods

The Maya and Aztecs shared beliefs and ideas. Both gave human sacrifices to their gods.

WOW!

Only three or four Mayan books have survived. Spanish conquistadors burned the rest.

REVOLUTIONS

When explorers rediscovered Mayan architecture, knowledge and art centuries later, people had to rethink their ideas about native peoples.

ATTACK ON LINDISFARNE

Lindisfarne is a tiny island off the coast of northeast England. It is famous for two things: the beautiful Bible produced by the monks in its monastery around 700 CE; and the savage attack on that monastery by Viking raiders in 793 CE. For the English, the raid marked the start of the Viking Age.

As raids became more commonplace, the sight of a Viking ship's scary, dragon-shaped prow struck terror into all who saw it.

These are the ruins of the monastery on Lindisfarne, which was looted by Vikings in 793 CE.

NEED TO KNOW

VIP St Aidan (c. 590 to 651 CE) brought Christianity to Northumbria (now northern England and southeast Scotland).

The Vikings were people from Scandinavia — the part of northern Europe that now makes up the countries of Denmark, Norway and Sweden.

The monastery on Lindisfarne was founded by the Irish monk St Aidan before 634 CE.

Viking raids died out after the Scandinavians became Christian. The last one on England was in 1153, and the last on Scotland was in 1263.

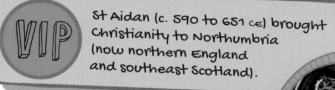

OFF TO NEW LANDS

There was rich farmland and good fishing around the coasts of Scandinavia, but inland the climate was harsh and the soil poor. Viking inheritance customs meant that when a father died, his land was shared equally between his sons. Soon, families were unable to produce enough food for themselves. Vikings took to the seas to trade, raid and settle in new lands.

WOW!

In Old Norse, —by meant 'town' and —thorpe meant 'village' or 'farmstead'. Look out for these in English place names, for example Grimsby and Scunthorpe.

Celtic cross

RICH PICKINGS

When the Vikings began to raid northern Europe, the Christian church was growing rich. Its monasteries and churches contained precious treasures but were poorly defended. The Vikings looted what they could to keep for themselves or to trade. They also took slaves. Not all Vikings were violent warriors, however. Most were well-travelled traders or peaceful settlers.

Medieval books were often handwritten by monks and intricately decorated. These pages are all from the Lindisfarne Gospels.

St Matthew

Page from The Gospel of St John

St Mark

REVOLUTIONS

The Vikings gave the Christian church a common enemy to fear. However, they also carried out important trade across Europe.

ISLAMIC WORLD

The Muslim era began during the life of Muhammad, a prophet. His revelations from Allah (God) are contained in the Islamic holy book, the Qur'an. After Muhammad's death, Islamic armies spread out from Arabia. Soon the Islamic world stretched from Spain to Central Asia.

The Muslims invaded Spain in 711 CE. This beautiful Spanish Qur'an was produced in the 1200s.

This is a page from a 14th-century Qur'an produced in Cairo, Egypt.

Muhammad's name in Arabic writing

Muhammad began receiving messages from Allah in 610 CE, aged about 40.

NEED TO KNOW

When Muhammad died in 632 CE, his father-in-law Abu Bakr became caliph (the leader of Islam).

Abu Bakr and his three successors are known as the 'rightly guided caliphs'. They were all elected or chosen.

The Umayyads were the first dynasty of caliphs — leaders by inheritance. They led the Islamic world from 661 to 750 CE.

HOLY CITIES

The three holiest cities in Islam
are Mecca, Jerusalem and Medina.
Mecca was Muhammad's home town.
In 620 CE angels transported Muhammad
to Jerusalem on his famous 'Night
Journey'. Muhammad fled to Medina
in 622 CE, after being persecuted by
the people of Mecca.

Muhammad said he visited Allah
up in heaven on his Night Journey.
This building, the Dome of the
Rock, was built around the
rock he went up there from.

The Dome of the Rock was
completed in 691 CE, but the blue
tiles were added in the 1500s.

SCHOLARSHIP AND LEARNING

Muslim scholars studied philosophy, maths,
medicine and astronomy. They translated ancient
works, for example from Greece and India,
and expanded on what they learned.
The 13th-century stargazer Nasir
al-Din Tusi was one of the greatest
astronomers of all time.

These drawings are by
the scholar al-Biruni,
who explained the
phases of the Moon.

WOW!
Muslims are expected
to make a pilgrimage
to Mecca at least
once in their
lifetime.

Tusi with the four men who set
up his observatory at Maragheh,
a city in what is now Iran

REVOLUTIONS

As Islam spread, so
did Muslim knowledge.
Even today, Arabic
numerals are still
the standard in
mathematics all
over the world.

TOUGH TIMES IN EUROPE

Life was tough in the Middle Ages - especially for the peasants. They were the workers who farmed the land. They worked for a lord, or knight, who gave them a little land for themselves as payment. Most of them struggled to grow enough food to support their families.

Reeve

These peasants are cutting corn. The reeve (one of the lord's officials) checks no one steals any produce.

The knight received his land and castle from the king. In return, he had to fight in the king's wars.

VIP

Wat Tyler led the Peasants' Revolt in England, but was killed by one of the king's men.

NEED TO KNOW

Despite its name, the Hundred Years' War between England and France lasted more than **100** years, from **1337** to **1453**.

The plague swept through Europe between **1347** and **1350**. It killed at least a third of the population.

In England, life became so difficult for peasants that they rebelled in **1381**. But when their leader was killed, they all went back to their homes.

THE BLACK DEATH

Medieval people did not have great medical knowhow. Many died of simple wounds or viruses. Thousands more died in wars and famines. The worst killer was the plague, or Black Death.

People carrying away the wrapped-up bodies of plague victims

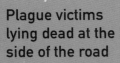

Plague victims lying dead at the side of the road

A plague doctor

OFF TO FIGHT

Wars were another problem. Kings and emperors wanted to capture as much land for themselves as possible. Around 3.5 million men died in the Hundred Years' War between England and France.

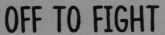

WOW!

The average life expectancy in the Middle Ages was only about 30 years.

About 2,000 French soldiers died in the Battle of Crécy (1346).

REVOLUTIONS

The system of peasants farming for lords and lords fighting for kings was hard. As towns grew, this way of doing things died out. People paid taxes and became free citizens.

CHANGES IN CHINA

Two royal families ruled medieval China: the Tang (618 to 907 CE) and the Song (960 CE to 1279). The time of the Tang emperors is called China's Golden Age. New inventions and technologies appeared, from clocks to printing. There was trade along the Silk Road.

The first Tang emperor was Gaozu. He seized power in 618 CE.

This cave painting was made in the 900s CE at a desert oasis along the Silk Road. It shows Buddhist monasteries from Tang times.

NEED TO KNOW

VIP Empress Wu Zetian was a strong Tang ruler. She reigned from 690 to 705 CE.

The Tang ruled China from **618** to **907** CE. Tang merchants travelled into Central Asia along the Silk Road.

The Tang grew weak and their dynasty ended. There was civil war until Taizu reunited China in **960** CE. He was the first Song emperor.

Mongol warriors conquered Central Asia and China during the **1200s**. Kublai Khan finally defeated the Song in **1279**.

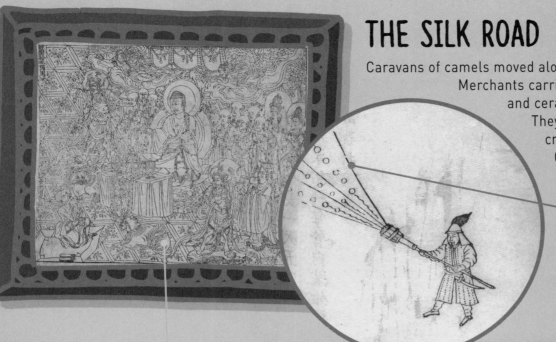

THE SILK ROAD

Caravans of camels moved along the Silk Road. Merchants carried silk, tea, paper and ceramics from China. They brought glass, jade, crystal and cotton from Central Asia.

Like silk, gunpowder was a Chinese invention — and how to make it was a closely guarded secret.

The Tang produced the oldest printed book. The *Diamond Sutra* (868 CE) is printed on a paper scroll.

THE GREAT KHAN

Genghis Khan was the first great Mongol leader. He united the Mongol tribes and moved east, taking territory as he went. He captured parts of China, but his grandson Kublai Khan finally conquered it. He pronounced himself emperor in 1271 and defeated the Song eight years later.

Genghis Khan sits on a mat surrounded by his sons.

WOW!

Kublai Khan was the first non-Chinese emperor to conquer all of China.

REVOLUTIONS

Vast and powerful, medieval China produced some amazing technologies and inventions — when it was stable and united, that is!

SAMURAI WARS

In the 12th century, two samurai (warrior) clans struggled for control of Japan. The conflict finally ended at a decisive naval battle on 24 April 1185, where the Minamoto family defeated the Taira clan. Minamoto Yoritomo went on to become Japan's first shogun, or 'supreme military commander'.

This 17th-century scroll shows Minamoto warriors defending their battlements as Taira forces attack.

The Battle of Dan-no-Oura

Red standards flown by the Taira

When the Taira realised they had lost, they all jumped into the sea — it was more honourable to drown than surrender.

NEED TO KNOW

VIP

Minamoto Yoritomo was the first of his family to rule as shogun, from 1192 to 1199.

During the Heian period (794 CE to 1185), the most influential family in Japan was the Fujiwara clan. It controlled the emperor and his court.

From 1155 onwards, there were civil wars and rebellions. The Taira family seized power.

The Minamoto clan defeated the Taira at the Battle of Dan-no-Oura (1185). They ruled as shoguns for more than 140 years.

BROTHERLY LOVE?

Minamoto Yoritomo was helped to power by his brother Yoshitsune, who became his best general. But as shogun, he worried that Yoshitsune might become a threat. Yoritomo sent men to kill Yoshitsune.

After four years on the run, Yoshitsune eventually committed suicide rather than give himself up!

Yoshitsune and a friend defend themselves against the shogun's men.

Kyoto was built to look like Chang'an, China's capital in the time of the Tang dynasty (618 to 907 CE).

KYOTO AND OTHER CITIES

Japan's imperial court had moved to Kyoto in the 8th century CE and it stayed there until the 19th century. The shoguns had their own centres of power. Minamoto Yoritomo ruled from the coastal town of Kamakura.

The shoguns — not the emperors — were the real power in Japan for hundreds of years. Samurai were the 'knights' who served them, and they had strict codes of honour.

1350 - 1850

GREATER HORIZONS

As the Middle Ages drew to a close, knowledge of other parts of the world began to grow. News of great empires in Africa and Asia reached European ears. China led the way in exploration in the early 1400s, but soon other nations were sending out expeditions to find new lands.

THE WORLD ... AND BEYOND!

During this Age of Exploration, the Americas and Australasia were discovered and new, faster ships brought greater trade. The world shrank, but scientific knowledge expanded. Workings of the world that had once been mysteries could now be explained. Scientists found out about forces such as gravity, were able to look inside the human body and found out more about our place in space.

Flemish mapmaker Gerardus Mercator made the first world map that took account of Earth being round in 1569. It was a huge help to sailors.

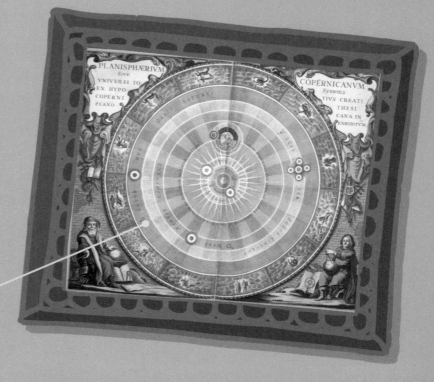

In 1543, Polish astronomer Nicolaus Copernicus said that the Sun, not the Earth, was at the centre of the solar system.

GERARDI MERCATORIS RVPELMVNDANI EFFIGIEM ANNOR.
DVORVM ET SEX — AGINTA, SVI ERGA IPSVM STVDII
CAVSA DEPINGI CVRABAT FRANC. HOG. CIƆ IƆ LXXIV.

AFRICAN RICHES

In 1324 Mansa Musa, a ruler from West Africa, went on a pilgrimage to Mecca. His caravans included tens of thousands of people and slaves. There were hundreds of servants, dressed in the finest silks and carrying staffs of solid gold. Mansa Musa's mind-boggling wealth amazed everyone.

This map from 1375 shows Mansa Musa holding a ball of gold, and seated on a gold throne.

Mansa Musa ruled Mali, on the southern edge of the Sahara. His wealth came from trade in gold, salt and slaves.

NEED TO KNOW

VIP

Mansa Musa ruled Mali from from 1312 to 1337.

The kingdom of Ghana was another important power in medieval West Africa. It was at its height between **750** ce and **1075**.

Songhai was originally part of the Mali empire. It became independent in the **1430s** and grew into one of the largest states in African history.

Benin was a city-state in West Africa. From the **1400s**, it controlled trade between Europeans on the coast and people inland.

Cape Bojador

This 16th-century chart shows the coastline of West Africa.

Timbuktu was part of the Mali empire and, later, the Songhai empire.

Europeans established trading posts along the coast.

EUROPEAN EXPLORATIONS

During the 1400s, Europeans began trying to find a sea route around Africa to Asia. In 1434, Portuguese Gil Eanes was the first to navigate around bulging Cape Bojador, a part of the West African coast that Europeans had never managed to sail around before. Forty-four years later Portuguese navigator Bartolomeu Dias rounded the southern tip of Africa.

GREAT ZIMBABWE

Portuguese explorers brought back tales of a wealthy empire that had flourished across southern African from the 12th to 15th centuries. Great Zimbabwe had grown rich from gold and ivory, trading with civilisations as far away as Persia and China.

These are ruins of the Great Enclosure, the walled palace at Great Zimbabwe where the emperor and his family lived.

Some parts of the walls were 11 m (36 ft) high.

Great Zimbabwe covered an area of 722 ha (1,780 acres) and was home to up to 20,000 people.

REVOLUTIONS

A number of great African empires flourished in medieval times. Mali was very important in allowing the spread of Islam in Africa.

BABUR THE TIGER

In 1526 a Mongol warlord called Babur conquered northern India. He founded the powerful Mughal dynasty that ruled India for more than 300 years. The Mughal empire was largest during the reign of Aurangzeb (1658 to 1707), when it covered most of southern Asia.

Babur defeated Sultan Ibrahim Lodi, ruler of northern India, at the Battle of Panipat in April 1526.

Babur, whose name means 'tiger', was descended from Genghis Khan.

NEED TO KNOW

VIP

During his reign, Shah Jahan coped with famines, rebellions and wars.

Babur's grandson, Akbar the Great, was the third Mughal emperor. He ruled from **1556** to **1605**.

Akbar's son, Jahangir, ruled from **1605** to **1627**. He expanded the empire and made it more stable.

Jahangir's son, Shah Jahan, is remembered for his amazing buildings. He ruled from **1628** to **1658**.

A WAY OF LIFE

The Mughals were Muslims, but Emperor Akbar was interested in learning about Indian beliefs, too. He became so interested in Jainism that he eventually gave up hunting and eating meat. Jains do not harm any living things.

Akbar tells his courtiers that they must not kill animals any more.

WOW!

More than 20,000 workers and 1,000 elephants helped to build the Taj Mahal.

THE TAJ MAHAL

The Mughals had their own style of building. The most famous example is the Taj Mahal. The fifth Mughal emperor Shah Jahan built it as a tomb for his wife Mumtaz Mahal. It took more than 20 years to build.

The Taj Mahal was built from dazzling white marble.

Splendid garden in front of the tomb

REVOLUTIONS

Babur was the first of a line of emperors that ruled India for centuries. They created beautiful art and monuments.

INSPIRED BY THE PAST

In the 1400s and 1500s, there was a great flowering of talent in Europe, especially in Italian city-states such as Florence and Venice. The rich Medici family ruled Florence. They showed off their wealth and power by paying the best artists of the day to produce beautiful pieces.

The Medici palace, Florence

The Virgin Mary visits her cousin Elizabeth – but instead of being in Judah, they are in Florence.

Venice was an important trading port.

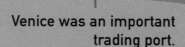

VIP

Cosimo de' Medici ruled Florence from 1434 to 1464.

NEED TO KNOW

Donatello (c.1386 to 1466) was one of the earliest Renaissance artists in Florence. He had support from the first Medici ruler, Cosimo.

Leonardo da Vinci (1452 to 1519) grew up in Florence. His most famous paintings are The Last Supper and the Mona Lisa.

Michelangelo worked in Florence and Rome. He produced some of the finest paintings and sculptures of the Renaissance.

LOOKING TO THE PAST

This time in European history is known as the Renaissance or 'rebirth'. Artists and architects studied the styles of ancient Greece and Rome and then produced their own beautiful works. Thinkers and scientists came up with new ideas, inspired by ancient texts.

Head of a woman (c. 1475), by Andrea del Verrocchio

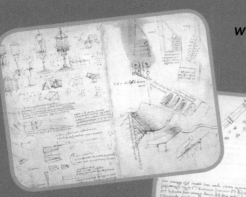

Leonardo's backwards mirror writing

Renaissance artists wanted their work to be as true to life as possible.

Thinker Leonardo da Vinci crammed his notebooks with ideas about machines and forces, gravity and motion, astronomy and geometry.

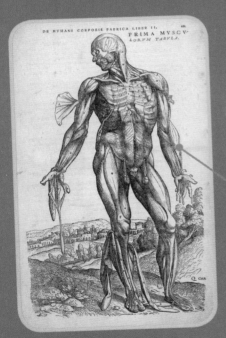

This sketch by the Renaissance anatomist Vesalius shows the body's main muscles.

WOW!

Leonardo da Vinci sketched inventions that were ahead of their time — such as a working helicopter!

NEW DISCOVERIES

The Renaissance thirst for knowledge led to greater understanding in all sorts of areas, from astronomy to anatomy. A Belgian-born doctor, Andreas Vesalius, performed the first dissections of the human body. He published a book about its workings in 1543.

REVOLUTIONS

Renaissance scientists laid the groundwork for many aspects of the modern world, from engineering to our understanding of space. Renaissance art has inspired and uplifted countless generations.

THE FALL OF CONSTANTINOPLE

In 1453, Sultan Mehmed II besieged Constantinople, capital of the 1,000-year-old Byzantine empire. His army's state-of-the-art iron siege cannons allowed him to conquer the city in just three months. The Turks' territory had reached the fringes of Europe.

Constantinople fell to the Ottoman Turks in August 1453.

Mehmed II 'the Conqueror' led more than 25 military campaigns. He was ruler from 1444 to 1446 and again from 1451 to 1481.

VIP

Mehmed II's great-great-great-great grandfather was Osman I (right), founder of the Ottoman dynasty.

NEED TO KNOW

The Roman empire split into two in 285 CE. The eastern half became the powerful Byzantine empire. It was Christian.

In 1300, Muslim ruler Osman I established a small state in Anatolia (now Turkey), on the edge of the Byzantine empire. His descendants would rule Turkey for more than 600 years.

At the Battle of Kosovo in 1389, the Ottomans reduced the Byzantine empire to a small area around Constantinople.

HEIGHT OF POWER

Suleiman I ruled longer than any other Ottoman sultan – 46 years. During his reign, the Ottoman empire reached its height. It stretched from Hungary to the Arabian Gulf and from the Crimea to Algiers. But Suleiman was defeated when he tried to take Vienna, Austria, in 1529. Christian Europe realised that the Ottomans were not unstoppable after all!

Suleiman I 'the Magnificent'

Ottoman general Lala Mustafa Pasha

WOW!

Between 1514 and 1823, the Ottomans fought eight wars against the Persians.

The Ottomans parade before the walls of Persian-controlled Tiflis (now Tbilisi) in the Caucasus in 1578.

STRUGGLES IN THE EAST

On their eastern borders, the Ottomans came into conflict with the powerful rulers of Persia (now Iran). They battled for control of eastern Anatolia, the Caucasus and Mesopotamia (now Iraq).

REVOLUTIONS

Constantinople (modern-day Istanbul) was the meeting place of east and west, and the Ottomans controlled all trade through it. They ruled until 1922.

SETTLING A NEW CONTINENT

In 1492 the Italian-born explorer Christopher Columbus was looking for a new sea route to Asia when he accidentally 'discovered' the Americas. He claimed land for the Spanish king and queen, who were funding his voyage. Soon other European powers were rushing to the New World, too.

The first land in the Americas that Columbus spotted was probably San Salvador in the Bahamas.

Columbus took three ships on his first voyage to the New World.

King Ferdinand of Spain

Christopher Columbus 'discovered' the Americas in 1492.

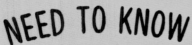

NEED TO KNOW

VIP

Spanish conquistadors included Hernán Cortés, who defeated the Aztecs by **1522**, and Francisco Vásquez de Coronado, who explored the southwestern United States in the **1540s**.

The first British colony in North America was on Roanoke Island, North Carolina. It was founded by Sir Walter Raleigh in **1585**.

The United States declared its independence in **1776**. Huge areas of the continent were still Spanish, French and British colonies until the early **1800s**.

BRITISH COLONIES

The first British colony, on Roanoke Island, was abandoned within five years, probably because of attacks by Native Americans. However, soon there were British settlements up and down the east coast. In 1620, Puritans from England reached Massachusetts. These Pilgrim Fathers set up a colony where they could practise their religion freely.

This engraving of a Native American town is based on a painting by one of the early English colonists, John White.

Native Americans hunting deer

INDEPENDENCE!

East-coast colonists became unhappy paying taxes to the British king so far away. From 1775 to 1781 they fought for their independence. They won, and a new nation was born – the United States of America.

WOW!

Explorer Sir Walter Raleigh named the Roanoke colony 'Virginia' after Queen Elizabeth I, who was known as the Virgin Queen.

In 1773, colonists in Boston threw precious crates of tea into the sea as a protest against taxes.

REVOLUTIONS

The Americans signed their Declaration of Independence on 4 July 1776.

When it was formed in the 1770s, the United States was a small collection of former colonies. Today, it is a world superpower.

IMPROVING INDUSTRY

In 1709, the owner of the Coalbrookdale foundry in northern England began to use a new method for making iron. By burning coke (a purer form of coal) in his furnace, he could achieve higher temperatures, and produce purer iron. It was the start of the Industrial Revolution.

The foundry at Coalbrookdale made the first steam engine cylinders and the first rails for the railways.

Industry needed coal. Men, women and children worked in dangerous conditions in underground mines.

Scottish inventor James Watt improved Newcomen's steam engine in 1781.

VIP

NEED TO KNOW

Thomas Newcomen built the first simple steam engine in **1712**. It was designed to pump out water from mines.

Inventions to help cotton spinning included James Hargreaves' spinning jenny (**1764**) and Richard Arkwright's water-powered spinning frame (**1771**).

Richard Trevithick demonstrated the first steam railway engine in **1804**. By **1825** England had the first public railway.

FIRST FACTORIES

Britain had all the ingredients for industry – raw materials, water, iron and coal. Its factories began to mass-produce goods such as textiles, ceramics, tools and machinery. Instead of farming, most ordinary people began to work in factories or down mines. Children had to work as well as adults.

Children going to work in a cotton mill

Inside a cotton mill

WOW!

There were no laws to protect factory workers until the 19th century.

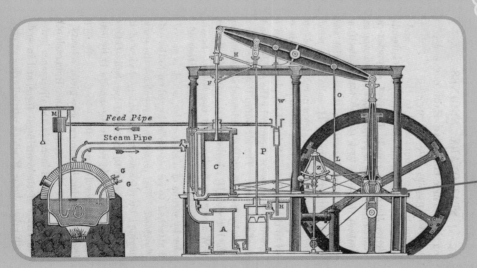

A diagram of a steam engine

Feed Pipe
Steam Pipe

STEAM POWER

In 1776, James Watt revolutionised manufacturing by creating a steam engine that could power machines. In the following century this engine would be used to build the first trains (1804) and steamships (1807).

REVOLUTIONS

The Industrial Revolution changed society as people moved from the countryside to towns and cities. The steam engine made travel faster and the world became a smaller place.

1850 – 1950

BIRTH OF THE MODERN WORLD

During the 19th century, European nations grew their empires to their largest extents. At the same time, the United States gained new territory until it covered much of its continent. In the 20th century, two world wars changed everything, and many new nations were born.

NEW TECHNOLOGIES

The world wars were deadlier than any other conflicts in human history. That was partly because of weaponry and other new technologies that made warfare more efficient. Trains, cars and aeroplanes, telephones and radio all appeared in the 19th and early 20th centuries. In today's digital age it is hard to imagine what an enormous impact they had by improving communications and making the world a smaller place.

Armoured tanks like this one were first used during World War I.

A 3.069-km (1,907-mile) railway connected the United States' east and west coasts from 1869.

XXXXXXXXXXXXXXXXXXX

BATTLE OF THE LITTLE BIGHORN

Following the United States' independence, Native Americans were forced off their lands to make way for settlers. This policy led to massacres and wars. In the Black Hills War (1876 to 1877), Lakota and Cheyenne refused to give up ancestral lands in Dakota.

The largest battle of the Black Hills War took place at the Little Bighorn river, Montana. Up to 2,500 Native Americans faced 650 US soldiers and killed almost half of them.

WOW!

Between 1800 and 1890, the number of Native Americans in the United States fell from 600,000 to 250,000.

General George Custer died at the Battle of the Little Bighorn.

NEED TO KNOW

VIP Lakota leader Sitting Bull foresaw the Native American victory at the Little Bighorn in a vision.

The United States declared independence from Britain in **1776** and won it in **1783**.

In the American Civil War (**1861** to **1865**), the northern (Union) states defeated the southern (Confederate) ones. Native Americans fought on both sides.

The Black Hills War was one of the Sioux Wars — conflicts between the US government and different Sioux tribes that took place between **1854** and **1890**.

PLAINS INDIANS

Native American tribes on the Great Plains, such as the Lakota, Dakota and the Arikara, lived in tepees for some of the year, while they were hunting buffalo. The arrival of white settlers ended this traditional way of life. The Native Americans were forced onto reservations.

Bear's Belly, Arikara

Yellow Horse, Yanktonai Dakota

Jack Red Cloud, Oglala Lakota

THE CIVIL WAR

While the American Indian wars were going on, trouble was brewing between the states. Northern ones wanted to end slavery, but southern ones did not. The four-year Civil War cost the US government more than $6 billion. It came out of the war with very little money to help Indians who were losing their land.

Gettysburg was the deadliest Civil War battle. It lasted just three days, but more than 50,000 soldiers were killed.

Abraham Lincoln was president during the Civil War.

REVOLUTIONS

The United States and its people were changed forever by wars in the 1800s. African American slaves were freed at the end of the Civil War. Native Americans, however, lost their land and way of life.

SCRAMBLE FOR AFRICA

In 1884, there was a conference in Berlin, Germany, about the future of Africa. No Africans were invited - instead, European leaders set out ways that they could claim Africa's land and precious resources. They split the continent into 50 colonies.

WOW!

In 1870, Europeans ruled 10 per cent of Africa; in 1900, they ruled 90 per cent.

Otto von Bismarck, the German chancellor

This cartoon of the Berlin Conference shows Africa being sliced up and shared out like a cake.

By 1898, Africa's colonies belonged mostly to the French (pink), English (yellow), Germans (green) and Portuguese (purple).

King Leopold II of Belgium created Congo Free State in Central Africa, so he could rule as its king.

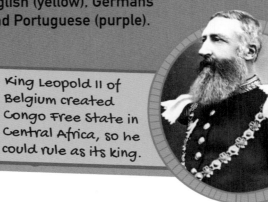

NEED TO KNOW

In **1882**, Egypt became part of the British empire. By **1900**, Britain ruled almost one-third of Africa's population.

The Berlin Conference was held between **1884** and **1885**. Fourteen European nations took part.

South Africa was one of the first states to gain independence from European rule, in **1910**. Angola was one of the last, in **1975**.

In 1849 Livingstone visited Lake Ngami, one of Africa's largest lakes.

Livingstone and one of his sons

MAPPING THE CONTINENT

Explorers and missionaries helped to map the African interior and find its reserves of gold and other minerals. Scottish missionary David Livingstone traced most of the route of the Nile, for example.

In 1871 Livingstone travelled along the Ruzizi river in Tanzania with fellow-explorer Henry Stanley.

This engraving of an Ashanti festival dates to 1818.

GHANA'S STORY

Around 1800, what is now Ghana, West Africa, was part of the Ashanti kingdom – apart from its coast, where European traders dealt in gold and slaves. Over the next century, Britain took over the Gold Coast ports, as well as the inland territory of the Ashanti. Ghana did not become independent from Britain until 1957.

REVOLUTIONS

European competition for Africa's resources caused harm. New borders separated some peoples and bunched others together randomly, resulting in bitter conflict.

A WORLD AT WAR

On 28 June 1914, a terrorist shot dead Archduke Franz Ferdinand, the heir to the Austrian-Hungarian throne, and his wife Sophie. He wanted to draw attention to his cause, Bosnian independence. This single act triggered a four-year war that eventually spread over the whole world and killed more than 20 million people.

There were complicated loyalties between the different nations of Europe. Soon they were all involved in the war.

Franz Ferdinand would have been the next Austrian-Hungarian emperor. To avenge his death, Austria-Hungary declared war on Serbia.

NEED TO KNOW

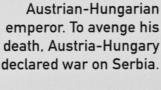

VIP Wilhelm II was emperor of Germany during World War I.

The Central Powers were Austria-Hungary, Germany, Bulgaria and the Ottoman empire.

The Allies were Serbia, Russia, France, the United Kingdom, Italy, Belgium, the United States and Japan.

At first, people thought the war would be over in a few months. It lasted four years, officially ending on **11 November 1918.**

LIFE ON THE WESTERN FRONT

The Central Powers faced fighting on two fronts in Europe, the Eastern and Western Fronts. Soldiers often fought from long, dug-out trenches. They attacked by going 'over the top' – running into the 'no man's land' between the enemy lines.

Weapons included shrapnel shells fired from artillery, hand grenades, rifles and bayonets.

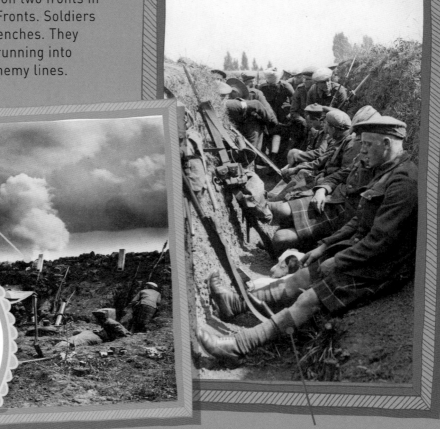

The bloodiest battle in the trenches was at the Somme in 1916. A million soldiers were killed or wounded.

Many soldiers lost their lives in the cramped, muddy trenches.

THESE WOMEN ARE DOING THEIR BIT

LEARN TO MAKE MUNITIONS

WOMEN AND THE WAR

Before the war, women had campaigned for equality. Now, while the men were away fighting, women had to do more jobs, for example on farms and in factories.

REVOLUTIONS

Women's contributions helped them to win the vote when the war ended. Europe's borders were redrawn after the war, and the losers had to pay crippling amounts of money to the winners. Both things helped lead to World War II.

REVOLUTION IN RUSSIA

The Russian Revolution was really two revolutions, which both happened in 1917. The February Revolution overthrew the Russian tsar and set up an emergency government to rule the country. In the October Revolution, the Communist Party took power.

Vladimir Lenin was the leader of the Communist Party.

Tsar Nicholas II was the last emperor of Russia. He ruled from 1894 to 1917.

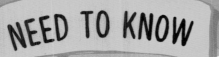

NEED TO KNOW

VIP Leon Trotsky was the commander of the Red Army.

Russia's part in World War I cost money, food and the lives of thousands. The people's desperation led to the February Revolution.

There was civil war from **1917** to **1922.** The Red Army fought for the Communists.

When the Reds won, the Communists founded a new republic, the Soviet Union. The Soviet Union lasted from **1922** to **1991.**

CIVIL WAR

The Communists seized power in the October Revolution, but many other groups wanted to take control of Russia. There were five years of unrest, uprisings and civil war. The biggest group against the Communists was called the White Army.

White Army forces on horseback

Lenin, Trotsky and other Communists

This propaganda poster was made to inspire people to fight the Communists. It shows their leaders being driven into hell.

WOW!

'Bolshy', meaning argumentative, comes from the Russian word Bolshevik. The Bolsheviks were people in Lenin's Communist Party.

Commune (settlement) is under a rainbow, the symbol of hope

A VISION OF HOPE

The Communists were inspired by the writings of the German thinker, Karl Marx. They wanted people to have shared ownership of their country and its resources, rather than it belonging to a few rich landowners.

The hammer and sickle symbolise industrial workers and farmworkers standing together.

REVOLUTIONS

The Soviet Union became one of the 20th century's most powerful nations. It achieved great things, but life for ordinary people remained hard.

THE TERRIBLE THIRTIES

The 1930s were a time of poverty and hardship. The period is known as the Great Depression. The main cause of the troubles was the collapse of the New York Stock Exchange in 1929. Companies went bankrupt and people lost their jobs. The effects soon spread around the world.

Unemployment and poverty were a problem everywhere. People protested and went on 'hunger marches'.

This powerful photo, taken in California in 1936, shows a farmworker with some of her children. The crop they came to pick has failed, and they have nowhere to go.

FOR A NEW DEAL

US President Roosevelt, elected in 1932, promised to fix the economy and create jobs.

NEED TO KNOW

VIP

During the **1920s**, many people had invested in stocks and shares. When prices suddenly dropped in **1929**, they lost everything.

Droughts in the early **1930s** led to food shortages and famines, especially in the Soviet Union.

In some ways, the outbreak of World War II in **1939** ended the Great Depression. People went to fight or make weapons.

WORTHLESS MONEY

Times were especially bad in Germany, which was being forced to pay money to the winners of World War I. The government tried to fix the problem by printing more money, but it just made things worse. Prices went through the roof.

Before the war, the highest German banknote was 1,000 marks (worth around £50). This 500-million-mark note was issued in 1923.

Money could not buy anything, so children used it as toys.

WOW!

In 1922 a loaf of bread cost 163 marks in Germany. By November 1923, it cost 200 billion marks.

Dust storms whipped up loose top soil and then dumped it.

THE DUST BOWL

In the American West, dust storms made unemployment even worse as people gave up their farms and moved to the cities to find work. The storms were caused by droughts and poor farming techniques. Crops failed and people went hungry.

REVOLUTIONS

People in Germany suffered very badly, and that helped Hitler rise to power. Elsewhere, the hardships people suffered made governments have to look at schemes for helping when citizens were sick or out of work.

ALL-OUT WAR ... AGAIN!

During the 1930s, Nazi leader Adolf Hitler had come to power in Germany. In 1939, his troops marched into Poland - the first step in his plan to conquer Europe. Britain and France declared war and soon all the major countries of the world were involved.

German troops march into Poland in September 1939.

Hitler led the Nazi Party, which believed that Germanic peoples were part of a superior race.

A British tank driver

NEED TO KNOW

VIP Winston Churchill was UK prime minister from 1940 to 1945 (and again from 1951 to 1955).

The three Axis powers were Germany, Italy and Japan. Bulgaria, Hungary, Romania, Yugoslavia and Thailand all fought on the Axis side, too.

The Allies were the United Kingdom, France and Poland. Other nations joined them, including the Soviet Union (now Russia), the United States and China.

World War II lasted six years and one day. It ended on **2 September 1945.**

PEARL HARBOR

On 7 December 1941 the Japanese carried out a surprise attack on the US fleet in Pearl Harbor, Hawaii. More than 2,400 Americans were killed. Until then, the United States had stayed out of the conflict. Now it joined the Allies and helped to win the war.

One of the US Navy's warships, USS *Arizona*, on fire in Pearl Harbor

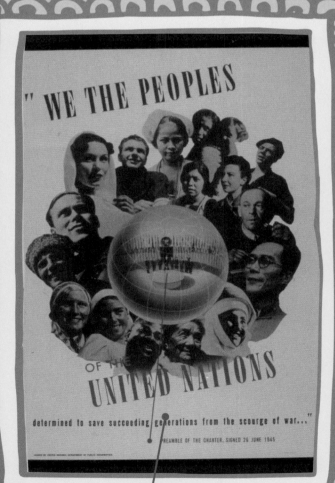

The United Nations was founded in 1945. Its aims were to avoid wars and protect people around the world.

WOW!

After the war, Germany was split into two nations. It stayed that way for 40 years.

THE AFTERMATH

Nazi ideas led to the horrors of the Holocaust, where Jews and others were murdered in death camps. Up to 11 million people were killed. In total, the war claimed nearly 70 million lives. World leaders formed the United Nations in the hope of avoiding the same horrors happening again.

REVOLUTIONS

It took time to repair the damage after the war. And the United States and Soviet Union did not trust each other, even though they had been allies.

GLOSSARY

afterlife
Life after death, often in another world, such as heaven or the underworld.

ally
A person or country who unites with another person or country against a common enemy.

anatomy
The scientific study of the structure of the body.

aqueduct
A bridge to support a canal transporting water.

artillery
The part of the army that uses large guns, mounted on wheels or tanks.

astronomy
The study of the stars and planets and their movements.

barbarian
The name given by the Romans to tribes outside the Roman empire.

bayonet
A blade that can be fixed to the end of a rifle and used for stabbing.

besiege
To surround a city or fortress and stop supplies entering or leaving it, with the aim of capturing it.

caliph
The title of a religious and political leader in the medieval Islamic world.

caravan
A group of people, usually riding camels, who travel together across desert country.

chancellor
The chief minister of the government in some European countries.

city-state
An independent state made up of a city and its surrounding countryside.

civil war
A war between opposing groups of people in the same country.

civilisation
A settled society that has developed a form of government, writing, organised religion, trade and great buildings.

classical
Relating to the period of the great ancient civilisations of Greece and Rome (between around 500 BCE to 500 CE).

colony
An area under the control of another state, or a group of people who have settled there.

cuneiform
Wedge-shaped symbols, a form of
writing developed in Mesopotamia.

democracy
A form of government based
on rule by the people, usually
through elected representatives.

dynasty
A royal family ruling a country
over successive generations.

empire
A group of lands or peoples brought
under the rule of one person
(emperor) or government.

evolve
To slowly change over time.

foundry
A factory or workshop where metal
or glass is made.

hieroglyphs
Picture symbols, a form of writing
used by many ancient peoples,
including the Egyptians and Maya.

hunter-gatherer
Someone who lives by hunting,
fishing and collecting wild foods.

observatory
A building for observing the stars
or weather.

philosophy
The study of existence and the
meaning of life.

relief
A carving that stands out
or is raised from the surface.

republic
A country without a hereditary ruler.

resource
Something that can be used to make
or do things.

revolt
To rebel and fight your
country's leaders.

shell
A metal case filled with explosive
and fired from a large gun.

shogun
One of the military leaders who ruled
Japan in the name of the emperor
between the 12th and 19th centuries.

shrapnel
Pieces of metal that scatter from an
exploding shell.

slave
A person who is held as the property
of another.

stylus
A pointed, stick-like implement
used for writing on wax tablets.

superpower
A very strong country that has more
power and influence than its allies.

INDEX

CREDITS

a = above, **b** = below, **c** = centre, **l** = left, **r** = right
All images © The British Library Board except:
Back cover – Pakal: Jabulon/Musée du Quai Branly, Paris; Plague doctor: Wellcome Images.
ArionEstar: 14b; © Patrick Aventurier - Caverne du Pont d'Arc: 7; Andreas F. Borchert: 24b; Jan Derk: 37b;
Jabulon/Musée du Quai Branly, Paris: 22b; Library of Congress, Washington D.C.: 2bl, 3al, 49, 50, 51c, 51b,
54l, 56b, 58r, 59b; Musée du Louvre, Paris: 9c; Amy McSimpson: 26b; Moldovita Monastery: 42a; O.Mustafin:
15c; NARA: 61; National Portrait Gallery, London: 46b; Nilfanion: 24c; Giovanni Dall'Orto/Agora Museum,
Athens: 12l; Pharos/Ernst Förstemann: 23a; Uffizi Gallery, Florence: 40b; Vassil/ Musée Mariemont,
Belgium: 9bl; Wellcome Images: 29al; www.123rf.com: 13b, 16a, 27a, 36c.

Hand-drawn design elements: Shutterstock, with thanks to AuraLux, Bisams, eaxx, Franzi, Krolia and Skokan Olena.
Typeset in Agent 'C' by Carl Leisegang, Lazing on a Sunny Afternoon by Frédéric Rich, Petit Four by Hanoded,
Gochi Hand by Huerta Tipográfica, La Belle Aurore by Kimberly Geswein and DIN Alternate.